A Holy Invitation

24 Day Advent Devotional

Reflections on Home, Hope & Hospitality

Tao Howard

A Holy Invitation: Reflections on Home, Hope & Hospitality
24 Day Advent Devotional

Published by Kainos Creative Studios Inc.
Barbados

www.kainoscs.com

Cover design, book design, production and illustration by
Kainos Creative Studios Inc.
Chapter images sourced at unsplash.com.
Copy edited by Ann Maxwell. Edits for accompanying audio by Dwayne Howard.

ISBN: 978-976-96568-0-2

*To the hearts and the homes where we've always
been welcome.*

To the ones who trimmed our tree with love.

Contents

...reaching backward to revere Him, and forward to receive Him...

Introduction

Despite being raised in the Christian church, Advent was foreign to me until recently. Yet, Christmas has always brought with it that childlike anticipation of something—or someone—coming (*adventus*), something to get excited about: whether it be a special day, a magical experience, an influx of visitors, or gifts, or food, a time of peace and goodwill...

For the believers in early centuries, Advent was without the trappings of modern-day commercialism. There was great celebration of the Savior born to us—the incarnation of a Messiah, and with equal gravitas, the expectation of His soon return—the King of the world. We find ourselves yet in the middle...reaching backward to revere Him, and forward to receive Him. He is our Guest of Honor, heralded with great eagerness: Oh come, Lord Jesus, come! And we are His eternal guests, invited into the Kingdom of His Father. Within this a theme emerges—a holy invitation to hospitality, near and dear to the heart of God, and here we want to focus for 24 days of Advent.

I realize that depending on the year you are reading this, the Advent period may be longer or shorter than the span of this devotional. I encourage you to take what you've read and make the other days ones of intentional prayer and practice.

Come along with me as I share thoughts of *Home*, *Hope* and *Hospitality*, of gifts that keep on giving, on receiving Him—and each other—with hospitality...as He teaches us to do.

Guest of Honour + Our Host

There are blooms men will never behold, species still sacred, cosmos unreached, revelations to be discovered, wonders without words attached to them.

Day One
The Extravagant Giver

A dear family member sent me an article about snowflakes. Her caption was a question: 'Why is God so *extra*?' I smiled, knowing exactly what she was talking about. The article explained how every single snowflake is absolute unmatched perfection—"tiny designs made of ice that are so individually unique, so detailed, and so spectacular."

I asked if she'd ever watched a rainforest documentary, or if she realizes how many species of bacteria exist on a dog's tongue. There are blooms men will never behold, species still sacred, cosmos unreached, revelations to be discovered, wonders without words attached to them. Why? God is nothing if not extravagant. He does nothing half-heartedly. He is the consummate Giver. His hands are neither short nor empty, and in His superfluity He gave us the Gift of His only-begotten Son and Holy Spirit. He gives Himself.

In *Beautiful Outlaw*, in a delightful chapter on Jesus's 'Extravagant Generosity', John Eldredge of Ransomed Heart Ministries puts it thus: "He is lavish with Himself...Jesus doesn't only give His life for mankind, He also gives His life to mankind." He asks us to give our lives as well.

The signs and miracles He performed were too many to be written down. The ways He works among us pass us by too rapidly to record them all. And surely we lack the vocabulary to contain Him. He is the Gift that keeps on giving. Oh how we want Him to come!

Prayerful Pause

Oh God, the Extravagant Giver, help us with grateful hearts as recipients of your boundless grace, to give only of our best to You and to others, withholding nothing. God, we look to You. Amen.

A Good Word James 1:17

Attention and Action _____

• *Was one thought or phrase from today's devotional illuminated as you were reading? Jot it here and what it called to mind for you.*

• *List three good gifts God has given you and take time to thank Him expressly for them now.*

• *In what ways has Holy Spirit revealed His extravagance to you this year, whether in character, provision, presence or in some other way?*

• *How can you show this aspect of Jesus's character to someone else? Write three tangible ideas you can put into action today.*

Creative Meditation

Use this verse space to highlight key words, doodle, color, circle, underline, whatever will help your heart recall the promise it contains.

Whatever is good and perfect is a gift coming down to us from God our Father, who created all the lights in the heavens. He never changes or casts a shifting shadow. James 1:17

Musical Notes "Give Thanks (Acoustic)" by DOE

Final Thoughts

In light of today's devotion, share your own reflection or declaration:
(I've included my own here as an example. Please write right over my words.)

Home is a good and perfect gift, even when it doesn't feel that way.

Hope is available to me without measure.

Hospitality is a privilege because it demonstrates Jesus.

Miracles are poised
at the end of our pause.

Day Two
Pause as Practice

Here we are at the beginning of December...again. The fittest heart grows faint at the thought of all that 'needs' to be done before the holidays come around. There is an arresting sense of overwhelm that can catch us up if we're not careful. Let's pause for a moment, early in the month, to put our priorities in appropriate order.

The ability to pause, and so ponder, is an underrated and underused gift. Mary's pause at the news from Gabriel produced a praise song instead of panic. Jesus paused, "It's not my time yet!" Wait turned to wonder, and water to wine. A pause ahead of the arrival of company—despite the flurry of activity to prepare for their coming—allows us to consider what will most make them comfortable. Whether it's a guest to our homes, or our hearts' Guest of Honor, with intentionality we create a place that says 'Welcome!' Miracles are poised at the end of our pause.

In your favorite Yuletide melody, it's the intervals of silence that make the music most potent. The absence of sound is a satisfying rest spot. That vacancy is meaningful. We've room to absorb the last musical phrase, before marinating in the next.

Christie Purifoy, in *Out of the Ordinary* podcast 54, spoke about the things she won't be doing for Christmas—among them the annual family photo card. "What might be more effort than it's worth this year?" she muses. It's a great question to ask ourselves if we would pare down the pandemonium and reach up for what is most precious in this season.

Prayerful Pause

Oh Preserver of Pause—the One who quiets our souls—help us grasp the moments between moments. Help us arrest our minds' anxieties, so we can plan our lives' activities in ways that are pleasing to You. Help us breathe, think, live. God, we look to You. Amen.

A Good Word Luke 2:19

Attention and Action ——————————————

• *Was one thought or phrase from today's devotional illuminated as you were reading? Jot it here and what it called to mind for you.*

• *Think about three ways you can fit an intentional pause into the busyness of this time of the year. Write them here as a reminder.*

• *What are your top three priorities for this Christmas period? Are they really in first place or are other matters pulling on your time and attention?*

• *To echo Christie, "What might be more effort than it's worth this year?" Jot down a few things that really won't make a difference if they aren't done.*

Creative Meditation _____

Use this verse space to highlight key words, doodle, color, circle, underline, whatever will help your heart recall the promise it contains.

But Mary kept all these things in her heart and thought about them often. Luke 2:19

Musical Notes "God I Look to You" by Bethel Music

Final Thoughts _____

In light of today's devotion, share your own reflection or declaration:

Home _____

Hope _____

Hospitality _____

How can it be that a God so far above us would take up residence in the hearts of men, make His dwelling in our messes, delight to fill our day to day?

Day Three

Willingly With Us

Lift a diamond to the light and one or the other of its facets will catch your attention. In a similar way, the more we look at Jesus, the more fascinated we become. So far we've marveled at the God of fullness who can extract so much out of emptiness; we've spoken of the Savior who came, and the King who will soon return. He's the *Was* and the *Is To Come*, but what of the God who *Is*—is present, is available, is near—right now, God with us?

Let's look to Him now as *Immanuel*. In this Name, I've always found a deep and enduring comfort: the certainty of His promise like a sip of sweetened sorrel, warm like cocoa. How can it be that a God so far above us would take up residence in the hearts of men, make His dwelling in our messes, delight to fill our day to day? Who am I (as one psalmist said) that You are mindful of me?

Maybe this doesn't mean as much to people with cookie cutter Christmases—where all is calm, and all is bright (does this even exist?). I wish that every Noel could be a Hallmark family movie, but the hard fact is that sometimes the glistening smiles are mere plastic. The season may be marred by loss, with someone missing from the table. Or the people at the table, though sitting together, may really be miles apart. Others don't look forward to the festivities because they can't see farther ahead than where they are right this moment. The future doesn't feel merry, or filled with cheer. Ghosts of Christmas Past lurk. Troubles of Christmas Present loom. Maybe you feel like you're not ready for all December will bring.

Take comfort. God is with you, His keeping power is tangible, His love for you is irrevocable. He is closer now than ever before. He's willing and able to prove it.

Prayerful Pause _____

Immanuel, prove for us Your promise. When our hearts are overwhelmed, remind us You are the same yesterday, today and forever. God willingly with us, and we secure in You. Amen.

A Good Word Matthew 1:23

Attention and Action

• *Was one thought or phrase from today's devotional illuminated as you were reading? Jot it here and what it called to mind for you.*

• *Is it more important to you that you* feel *like God is with you? Or that you* know *that He is with you? Why?*

• *What does it mean to you to know that God is willingly with you— that no matter what this Christmas brings He is right there to bring you through it?*

• *God makes His presence felt through our love for one another. What can you go out of your way to do today to help someone experience God's love?*

Creative Meditation

Use this verse space to highlight key words, doodle, color, circle, underline, whatever will help your heart recall the promise it contains.

"Look! The virgin will conceive a child! She will give birth to a son, and they will call him Immanuel, which means 'God is with us.'"

Matthew 1:23

Musical Notes "Emmanuel, God With Us" by Amy Grant

Final Thoughts

In light of today's devotion, share your own reflection or declaration:

Home

Hope

Hospitality

She knew...
that the
bitter would
interlace the
sweet, that
pain and
pleasure oft
would meet...

Day Four

(Un)Invited

Is it just me or does Jesus's birth story read like a Netflix series?

Who was that stranger from last episode whispering with Mary in the olive grove? What will Joseph do when he finds out she's pregnant? Will they make it out of town with the baby before the killing starts? What's he pulling from that sack? A gun? No, just some bars of gold. And will Herod ever find out that his agents double crossed him?

As Mary gazed up at a glittering sky the night before Gabriel's visit, there was no way she could have foreseen all that would unfold. Even if she knew of the prophecies, she didn't know the prophecies were of *her*. Life can come at us suddenly; and change is an often uninvited guest.

It's easy to read the story knowing well of the happy ending, and take for granted the emotion, the uncertainty, the tumult wrapped up in this unexpected adventure. Suddenly, it was her. Ready or not. Mary did you know? She knew...that the bitter would interlace the sweet, that pain and pleasure oft would meet. She could either resist the change and miss the promise, or surrender to transition with faith's arms extended.

She clung to the One who is never caught by surprise, who held her life in His hands, and so we received Him and welcome Him still: Salve for our situations, Security in our suddenlies, Prince of Peace!

Prayerful Pause

Oh Prince of Peace, You will keep us in perfect peace when we fix our minds on You. We will remain where You remain, so we can weather any change. We surrender to Your suddenlies. Lead us into adventures with You. Amen.

A Good Word Isaiah 9:6, Matthew 1 & 2

Attention and Action ————————————————

• *Was one thought or phrase from today's devotional illuminated as you were reading? Jot it here and what it called to mind for you.*

• *How has life caught you by surprise this year? List some positive and negative suddenlies and how you dealt, or are dealing with them.*

• *Imagine how Mary would have felt to find out she was pregnant. Write a few words to her of encouragement and support.*

• *What does it look like to 'surrender with faith's arms extended'? What makes this easy or difficult for you in your own uncertain situations?*

Creative Meditation

Use this verse space to highlight key words, doodle, color, circle, underline, whatever will help your heart recall the promise it contains.

For a child is born to us, a son is given to us. The government will rest on his shoulders. And he will be called: Wonderful Counselor, Mighty God, Everlasting Father, Prince of Peace. Isaiah 9:6

Musical Notes "Peace" by Mikey Mercer and John Yarde

Final Thoughts

In light of today's devotion, share your own reflection or declaration:

Home

Hope

Hospitality

It's the nostalgia of nights around a feast for the senses, crammed into a little overweight suitcase. Love travels.

Day Five

A Piece of Heaven

Anyone who's lived away from home and received a care package of food from family knows what it feels like to explore the treasures inside. You can almost taste the flavors as the wrapping paper falls away. The aromas transport you across the miles and the warmth of each bite goes down to your toes It's a craving satisfied, but not just for tasty treats.

It's home away from home—a little piece of paradise come to stay. It's the thoughtfulness that added the raisins to the conkies, and made sure the sweet bread made the trip. It's the nostalgia of nights around a feast for the senses, crammed into a little overweight suitcase.

Love travels. It's all that you miss, only quasi-accessible; all that's dearest to your heart, far but not forgotten. It's a symbol of someone special somewhere desiring your presence. It's a reminder of where you've belonged all along.

Special delivery! Love arrived in a package called Jesus—an Ambassador of the place where we truly belong, a reminder of how desirable that eternal dwelling still is, and how much we are desired in return. O come, let us adore Him, taste and see that He is so good—our hope of heaven and home.

Prayerful Pause _____

Father, we thank you for the gift of Jesus. He is a symbol to us of Your unrelenting love. Your thoughts toward us are of a glorious future. We long to be with You. You long for us more. Amen.

A Good Word Psalm 34:8

Attention and Action _____

• *Was one thought or phrase from today's devotional illuminated as you were reading? Jot it here and what it called to mind for you.*

• *What are your favorite treats to receive in a care package and who is most likely to send you one?*

• *Where do you most feel a sense of belonging? Identify what it is about that place that lends that to you and share how you can lend that to someone else.*

• *Someone special desires your presence, and He sent His Holy Spirit to be with you. Take some time to sit in prayer and write whatever He tells you.*

Creative Meditation

Use this verse space to highlight key words, doodle, color, circle, underline, whatever will help your heart recall the promise it contains.

Taste and see that the Lord is good. Oh, the joys of those who take refuge in him! Even strong young lions sometimes go hungry, but those who trust in the Lord will lack no good thing.

Psalm 34:8,10

Musical Notes "You Are the Living Word" by Fred Hammond

Final Thoughts

In light of today's devotion, share your own reflection or declaration:

Home

Hope

Hospitality

Reflecting off each
other, shining
instruments
of His peace —
serving strangers,
strengthening each
other— sparkling
hospitality extended
in the gospel way.

Day Six

Lit

I look forward one day in the weeks ahead, to taking our boys for a walk to see all the wonderful lights and decorations in our neighborhood. Drive through now and the pieces all still line the lawns like shrapnel from an explosion in the nearest Holiday Shop. Melted snowmen wait for hot air to be blown into them. Sleighs and Santas sit propped in a corner. Nativity scenes lie out in various stages of disarray.

A few of the eager neighbors got started right after Thanksgiving. Gorgeous oversized ornaments hang from the wide reaching trees up the avenue. And ever so often I get nervous that a plane will mistake my neighbor's glowing front yard for a multicolored landing strip.

Some of the arrangements are so intricate that it will take days to get them all assembled. But what a joy to behold when everything's done and this house right here rivals the very next one. This is no competition though, it's camaraderie. Each one in the spirit of community contributing his bit of beauty to the whole.

That's how we too should be, surely, who bear the light of Christ to a darkened world. We've incandescent opportunity to reflect the Light of life in our speech, our behavior, in our attitudes, in our love. Reflecting off each other, shining instruments of His peace—serving strangers, strengthening each other—sparkling hospitality extended in the gospel way. In this people see Jesus, when what we've beheld, we become.

Prayerful Pause

Incomparable Light, we pray Your words back to You. May we all who contemplate Your glory with unveiled faces, be transformed into Your image with the ever-increasing glory that comes from You.

A Good Word 2 Corinthians 3:18

Attention and Action

• *Was one thought or phrase from today's devotional illuminated as you were reading? Jot it here and what it called to mind for you.*

• *In your neighborhood what are some of the ways you can tell that Christmas is around the corner?*

• *Look to Him now, for what we behold we become. For each area (speech, behavior, attitudes and love), share one way you can reflect the Light of life.*

• *What areas of your life do you need the Light of life and truth to shine into as we approach a new year? Ask for clarity and direction on the next few lines.*

Creative Meditation _____

Use this verse space to highlight key words, doodle, color, circle, underline, whatever will help your heart recall the promise it contains.

So all of us who have had that veil removed can see and reflect the glory of the Lord. And the Lord— who is the Spirit—makes us more and more like him as we are changed into his glorious image. 2 Corinthians 3:18

Musical Notes 'Beauty Beauty" by David Brymer

Final Thoughts _____
In light of today's devotion, share your own reflection or declaration:

Home _____

Hope _____

Hospitality _____

The shame and the taboo would still rest upon
their shoulders, but it was lightened by a
promised joy that was closer at hand than ever.

Day Seven

Script Changes

There's a dazzling lack of detail surrounding the birth of Jesus. For all we do know to be factual, there's much more our imaginations conjure. We fill the narrative with iconic lore, and beloved hymnal lyrics, with extra-biblical traditions tacked on to set the scene.

One thing we do understand is that Mary was heavily and probably visibly pregnant during her time in Bethlehem. We know this because while she was there, the time came for her to give birth. We also know that Mary and Joseph weren't yet married. The Scripture still refers to her as his betrothed when they went up to be registered. And we know that before the angel came to Joseph he was going to break off the engagement quietly. The seriousness of the circumstances didn't change, just because he adjusted his attitude about it. The shame and the taboo would still rest upon their shoulders, but it was lightened by a promised joy that was closer at hand than ever.

At the risk of doing exactly what I'm suggesting we don't do—read things into the story that aren't there—I do wonder. Was there no room for them in the inn? Or was there no room for *them* in the inn? Do you see the difference? Were those guest quarters of yore full as we assume? The census was being taken, after all. Or was there just no room for Mary and Joseph, because of the 'indecency' of their situation? Perhaps we will never be sure, but we can know this for certain. For those who feel displaced, unwanted or rejected, weighed down by embarrassment or isolation, there is a place in the heart and plan of God for you. He will never leave you destitute or desolate. There will always be a secure space called hope in Jesus Christ where you can finally lay your swaddled burdens down.

Prayerful Pause

Be Thou our Guardian and our peace, the Lifter of our heads. Thank you for having many plans in your heart concerning us. For all the circumstances we cannot change, we find solace and safety in You. Amen.

A Good Word Romans 8:1, Luke 2:1-6

Attention and Action _____

• *Was one thought or phrase from today's devotional illuminated as you were reading? Jot it here and what it called to mind for you.*

_____

_____

_____

_____

• *Were you ever far from home at Christmas or some other special time? Mention some of the ways you can create a home away from home.*

_____

_____

_____

_____

• *God's plans for us are good, but sometimes it feels like He changes the script on us. Ask Him to show you how He is working everything out for your good.*

_____

_____

_____

_____

• *Have you felt the wait of shame or isolation? Do you feel it now? Jesus Christ is your security; You belong to Him; you are accepted. Thank him here.*

_____

_____

_____

_____

Creative Meditation

Use this verse space to highlight key words, doodle, color, circle, underline, whatever will help your heart recall the promise it contains.

So now there is no condemnation for those who belong to Christ Jesus. And because you belong to him, the power of the life-giving Spirit has freed you from the power of sin that leads to death. Romans 8:1-2

Musical Notes "Face of God" by Phil Wickham

Final Thoughts

In light of today's devotion, share your own reflection or declaration:

Home

Hope

Hospitality

27

Gloria in excelsis Deo!

There they were, minding their own business, when an angel unzipped the darkness and stepped into the middle of their camp.

Day Eight

Entertaining Angels

The night was deliciously cool but a warm fire kept them cozy. The banter was about the usual: whatever wild animal had threatened the sheep that day, the distance to the next watering hole, talk of the family they had waiting at home. Someone struck up a song after the other one finished a story, someone pointed out how striking that one star looked in the canopy, and perhaps for another a little ennui was settling in.

There they were, minding their own business, when an angel unzipped the darkness and stepped into the middle of their camp. The glory of God lit up the night like a spotlight illuminates a stage, and they were terrified. But the angel was bringing comforting news that filled the air with anticipation. "Today your Savior was born...He is Christ, the Lord." Then, the first flash mob in history came out of almost nowhere—a light show of entertaining angels, in chorus praising God on high.

There you'll be, minding your own business, when someone steps out of obscurity and leans into your charity, at the most mundane or inconvenient of times. We're challenged, "*Remember to welcome strangers, because some who have done this were entertaining angels without knowing it.*' Whether or not to our immediate benefit, our bible tells us not to miss any opportunity to be hospitable, whether to our brothers and sisters, or those we've never encountered before. In so doing may they leave our presence, having come upon His presence/presents, and giving glory not to us, but to our God on high.

Prayerful Pause

Lord we want to see you glorified, in all things and at all times. We won't ignore your call to hospitality. When it feels uncomfortable, take us over and above and teach us the way of Love.

A Good Word Luke 2:10-11; Hebrews 13:2

Attention and Action

• *Was one thought or phrase from today's devotional illuminated as you were reading? Jot it here and what it called to mind for you.*

• *Have you ever seen a real angel? Recount the experience. If you haven't, write what you think it would be like to have such an encounter.*

• *Sometimes showing hospitality is inconvenient, costly or difficult. How can you push past these obstacles and take advantage of the opportunity?*

• *Describe a time when someone went out of their way to make you feel welcome or comfortable when you were a stranger or guest.*

Creative Meditation

Use this verse space to highlight key words, doodle, color, circle, underline, whatever will help your heart recall the promise it contains.

Don't forget to show hospitality to strangers, for some who have done this have entertained angels without realizing it!

Hebrews 13:2

Musical Notes "Way of Love" by Kingdom Arts Music featuring Tao Howard

Final Thoughts

In light of today's devotion, share your own reflection or declaration:

Home

Hope

Hospitality

Letting
go of old
perspectives,
and the
pressure we
put ourselves
under,
placemaking
the private as
much as the
public spaces
of our lives...

Day Nine

Perfect vs Peace

Do you think Mary and Joseph were expecting guests the night that Jesus was born? They may have cringed at the meagerness of their lodging; the inability to lay out a spread to welcome those who stumbled into their miracle. A hostess' nightmare is to find herself with unexpected company; she will always prefer time ahead to make sure everything is just right. Even if she is prepared enough to already have things in order, it's the little special touches that she prides herself on.

But there are just some events for which you cannot be prepared. This Steven Furtick quote rocked my world: "The enemy of your peace is your insistence on perfection." True on many levels, let's consider this. We can get really caught up around this time of the year trying to Mary Poppins everything and make it 'practically perfect in every way'. We treat our homes the way we treat ourselves going into January. New this, new that, new curtains, new resolutions. Out with the dusty unused old, and in with another looming list of to-dos.

It will never all be accomplished with exact precision, so can we focus more this year on perfecting our peace? Letting go of old perspectives, and the pressure we put ourselves under, placemaking the private as much as the public spaces of our lives—can we let Him set the standard as our hearts' Guest of Honor? When we do it His way, it's there we find our peace.

Prayerful Pause _____

God who calls us to be perfect as You are, help us keep only the pace that You set. You know that we are dust, and that our best intentions often lead to frustration. You will give us no more than we can bear, with perfect peace accompanying. And so we bless You. Amen.

A Good Word Psalm 103

Attention and Action _____

• *Was one thought or phrase from today's devotional illuminated as you were reading? Jot it here and what it called to mind for you.*

• *What old perspectives are you willing to let go of as the year closes? What new rhythms can you set in place to promote peace in heart and home?*

• *Have you ever had to deal with uninvited or unexpected guests? How did you handle it and how did it turn out in the end?*

• *Share any areas of your life where insistence on perfection by human standards is costing you peace of mind or stopping you from stepping out.*

Creative Meditation

Use this verse space to highlight key words, doodle, color, circle, underline, whatever will help your heart recall the promise it contains.

The Lord is like a father to his children, tender and compassionate to those who fear him. For he knows how weak we are; he remembers we are only dust. Psalm 103:13-14

Musical Notes "Find My Peace" by Naomi Raine

Final Thoughts

In light of today's devotion, share your own reflection or declaration:

Home

Hope

Hospitality

Sometimes all that's needed is a slow-working therapy: the right amounts of personal space, and time.

Day Ten

Songs, Space and Time

When I told my sons about my plan to take them lights-gazing, and one mentioned 'people singing outside the door with deadpan eyes', I realised: A. he thought I meant we'd be going caroling; B. it wasn't an idea he was fond of; and C. that maybe he had seen one crazy Christmas commercial too many. But the visual got me thinking...about ways we encroach on people's lives with our own, without even knowing it.

Melancholy takes its toll on many during the holidays. But noble intentions to the tune of "God Rest Ye Merry Gentlemen" can't fix those 'somethings' that dismay. It's not remedied by a Pentatonix playlist. So anxious to see the ones we love get past their pain, we approach them with blind eyes—albeit brimming with good cheer, but empty of sensitivity—willing them to warmth when a snowman is all they can be right now.

"Like one who takes away a garment in cold weather...is one who sings songs to a heavy heart." Why try to force them into your felicity? Sometimes all that's needed is a slow-working therapy: the right amounts of personal space, and time.

Put a coat around that snowman and remind him that you're there. Pray silently when they come to mind, or audibly when they allow it. Being hospitable this Season is just as much about what you *don't* do... and that may earn you the invitation, however reluctant, to something more.

Prayerful Pause

Wonderful Counsellor, help us know what is needed, whether a song to lift the spirits or the ministry of space and time. You fluently speak Love's languages; we are open to your leading. Amen.

A Good Word Proverbs 25:20

Attention and Action

• *Was one thought or phrase from today's devotional illuminated as you were reading? Jot it here and what it called to mind for you.*

• *Do you know anyone who is sad or lonely this Christmas? How can you support someone whose mood is less than magical by what you do or don't?*

• *Gary Chapman's 5 love languages are words of affirmation, receiving gifts, physical touch, acts of service and quality time. Which do you use most often?*

• *We all need a little space and time sometimes. Maybe you're the melancholy one. Pour your heart out on paper—songs, sorrows and everything in between.*

Creative Meditation

Use this verse space to highlight key words, doodle, color, circle, underline, whatever will help your heart recall the promise it contains.

Singing cheerful songs to a person with a heavy heart is like taking someone's coat in cold weather or pouring vinegar in a wound.

Proverbs 25:20

Musical Notes "All is Bright" by 116 feat. 1K Phew, Derek Minor & Wande

Final Thoughts

In light of today's devotion, share your own reflection or declaration:

Home

Hope

Hospitality

A public figure whether He liked it or not, Jesus was marked both by the circumstances of His birth and the weightiness of His calling.

Day Eleven
Marked

The shepherds would know Him when they saw him, swaddled and lying in a manger. The star would fix itself above Bethlehem and lead the Magi right to him. Simeon recognized Him. Anna did as well. Herod would have, if he could find Him. Distinguishing details always put our Savior in the spotlight. Jesus had a target on His back from the day He was born. Why do you think He often wanted His miracles and identity kept quiet?

Scholars identify at least 200 Messianic prophecies, many of which have already been fulfilled in the person of Jesus Christ. I've learnt from Lee Strobel's *The Case For Christ* that the chances of one person fulfilling just eight of those prophecies is one...in a hundred million billion. That's a scientifically proven 17 zeros in odds. Each time He stepped into the fullness of one it confirmed another. That doesn't help with staying under the radar.

A public figure whether He liked it or not, Jesus was marked both by the circumstances of His birth and the weightiness of His calling. And so are we. With indelible stains of rebirth and a call to carry our crosses, do we proudly bear in our bodies the marks of a courageous King? Can anyone tell that we've been with Jesus? Have we been marked by His presence in our lives?

Prayerful Pause

Jesus, You were a wanted man in more ways than one, but you never once abandoned Your calling. Give us the courage we need to bear Your image rightly. Mark us in modernity with eternity. Amen.

A Good Word Galatians 6:17, Acts 4:13

Attention and Action

• *Was one thought or phrase from today's devotional illuminated as you were reading? Jot it here and what it called to mind for you.*

• *Jesus was a* wanted *man in many ways. Think of some of the distinguishing characteristics that might have made Jesus's life and ministry very visible.*

• *Can anyone tell that you've been with Jesus? How are you making His presence a practice in your life? Is there room for improvement?*

• *How have you been marked by the presence of God in your life? Share some of the ways you have seen, heard or sensed Him since starting this devo series.*

Creative Meditation

Use this verse space to highlight key words, doodle, color, circle, underline, whatever will help your heart recall the promise it contains.

...they could see that they were ordinary men with no special training in the Scriptures. They also recognized them as men who had been with Jesus.

Acts 4:13

Musical Notes "Noel" by Chris Tomlin featuring Lauren Daigle

Final Thoughts

In light of today's devotion, share your own reflection or declaration:

Home

Hope

Hospitality

...both the poisonous and
pleasant factors of life
have supporting roles to
play in your story...

Day Twelve
Casting Call

Been thinking about Herod. And Lex Luthor. I have all boys in my home, you understand. Collective breaths had been held around here—for Christmas and the promise of no-school days—but also in anticipation of the long awaited "Crisis On Infinite Earths" crossover series on The CW Network. Heroes and antiheroes from across the multiverse would unite to stop The Anti-Monitor from destroying various Earths and all of reality.

With so much at stake there's understandable tension, but no more so—spoiler alert—than when Lex is beamed to their HQ in one of the episodes. Fans and heroes are confused. This is a villain; how is *he* going to help the situation? The Monitor's cryptic answer came: "Even he has his part to play..."

Enter King Herod. Tyrant. A proverbial slur on the story. About as nefarious as they come. To save Jesus's life the family skipped town for Egypt, remaining there until the threat was gone. God delivered Israel, He delivered Jesus, and He still rescues us from fear and bondage today.

Crisis has been averted because of a *plot twist* better known as God Incarnate. In the shadow of this Hero, Herod acted out his part in the feature length drama of God's Unfailing Love. As you see, both the poisonous and pleasant factors of life have supporting roles to play in your story. They're already rehearsing the scenes that will bring it to a good and glorious ending.

Prayerful Pause _____

Author and Finisher of our faith, you've written us into an adventure of epic proportions. But we know that all the action is working together for our good. When the curtain falls may Your name alone be in the credits. Amen.

A Good Word Romans 8:28, Jeremiah 29:11-12

Attention and Action ⎯⎯⎯⎯⎯⎯⎯⎯⎯⎯⎯⎯

• *Was one thought or phrase from today's devotional illuminated as you were reading? Jot it here and what it called to mind for you.*

• *It is so good to know that when we love God, all things work together for our good. Release whatever worries you've been holding in a few lines.*

• *Recount one story from your life where all hope was lost and you know for sure it had to be God who came through with deliverance on your behalf.*

• *What are you excited for this Christmas? What seasonal adventures (big or small) can you get into, or create for others to enjoy?*

Creative Meditation

Use this verse space to highlight key words, doodle, color, circle, underline, whatever will help your heart recall the promise it contains.

And we know that God causes everything to work together for the good of those who love God and are called according to his purpose for them. Romans 8:28

Musical Notes "King of Kings" by Hillsong Worship

Final Thoughts

In light of today's devotion, share your own reflection or declaration:

Home

Hope

Hospitality

...when is the last time your
soul felt its worth?

Day Thirteen

Felt Needs

Last night I just felt like I wanted to disconnect from the virtual, so I reached for the tangible...some paper and a pencil. Pausing from my writing, I absentmindedly flipped the pencil upside down and tapped it against my nose. I noted its even balance as I turned it in my hands, felt the coolness of the ferrule against the skin on my face, and inhaled the earthy potpourri of rubber and wood. It brought back happy feelings of childhood scribbling in my journal.

It's amazing what you notice when you take a little time to engage your senses, and it's easy to forget how something feels when you're not paying too much attention to it. Words from "Oh Holy Night" lingered on my tongue today, like when you read something 99 times and on the hundredth it arrests you with meaning. I asked myself—so now I ask you—when was the last time your soul *felt* its worth?

I won't linger too long now, but I want to remind you that sparing no expense, because of His great love for us, God gave the gift of His only begotten Son. He counted it worthwhile to make such a great sacrifice, so that we might have life and that in abundance. We are held in the highest esteem by the Highest Authority, and He invites us as kings to experience the sensory pleasures of His Kingdom. The best of these is to know Him for ourselves. Let this next few moments be your RSVP. The marks of divine encounter upon a human heart produce that which is profound, lasting and true. Fall on your knees. Embrace the thrill of hope. Your soul will rejoice in affirmation when He appears.

Prayerful Pause _____

Christ, You are Lord! We praise Your name forever, Your power and glory ever more proclaim. Our worth in Your eyes answers our souls' deepest needs. Thank You for Your great sacrifice of Love for us. Amen.

A Good Word   John 3:16

Attention and Action ————————————

• *Was one thought or phrase from today's devotional illuminated as you were reading? Jot it here and what it called to mind for you.*

—————————————————————————————
—————————————————————————————
—————————————————————————————
—————————————————————————————

• *How do you disconnect from the speed of a modern world? Recall your favorite time-tested methods for unplugging.*

—————————————————————————————
—————————————————————————————
—————————————————————————————
—————————————————————————————

• *RSVP in a few lines to Holy Spirit's invitation to divine encounter. Let Him know how much of a delight it is to be desired.*

—————————————————————————————
—————————————————————————————
—————————————————————————————
—————————————————————————————

• *When was the last time your soul felt its worth? In what ways does the King of Kings remind you of your exceeding value to Him?*

—————————————————————————————
—————————————————————————————
—————————————————————————————
—————————————————————————————

Creative Meditation

Use this verse space to highlight key words, doodle, color, circle, underline, whatever will help your heart recall the promise it contains.

For this is how
God loved the
world:
He gave his one
and only Son, so
that everyone who
believes in him will
not perish but have
eternal life. John 3:16

Musical Notes "O Holy Night" by Lauren Daigle

Final Thoughts

In light of today's devotion, share your own reflection or declaration:

Home

Hope

Hospitality

...there's a way
that time slows
down when
you're waiting
for something
special to
happen...

Day Fourteen
The Weight of the Wait

Ah Simeon! The Bible tells us this dear, devoted man was good and He was godly. He was waiting with great expectation for God to punctuate Israel's suffering with His glorious plan of salvation. We're told a very special detail - that the Holy Spirit was in Him, and God had promised that he would not die before he saw the promised Christ. Sure enough, one day he was blessed to hold the Messiah in his arms.

I imagine there were many opportunities for this faithful witness to lose hope that what he believed would come to pass. We are not told that he was old, but there's a way that time slows down when you're waiting for something special to happen. I wonder if each day he felt closer to the grave, weighed down by anxiety; or if he was so assured God's word would not fail that it only made him more ardent. Either way, waiting is never easy, but in this case it was blessed. In the face of the Life-Giver, Simeon was finally free to take the first of his dying breaths.

And so, blessed are they who do not yet see Him, who can't trace how He's working behind the scenes, who can't see what He's doing—but still they are waiting—holding onto promises, visions and dreams, who can't tell how things could possibly all work together; and yet with hope in a word spoken in due season, they believe....cling, hold, lean, trust, breathe.

Prayerful Pause

We are free from the weight of the wait, for Your burdens are wondrously light. In due season we will reap if we don't faint. Sustain us, Promise Keeper, we cling to your words of life, knowing that You have never failed. Amen.

A Good Word Luke 2:30-32

Attention and Action ——————————————

• *Was one thought or phrase from today's devotional illuminated as you were reading? Jot it here and what it called to mind for you.*

• *Imagine what it must have been like for Simeon to finally hold this great Promise close to him. What words might describe the experience?*

• *What are you holding on to with ardent faith? How are you keeping that faith alive as you wait?*

• *Lord, Your burdens are wondrously light, we lay our own heavy concerns down on the next few lines, and ask You to sustain us.*

Creative Meditation _____

Use this verse space to highlight key words, doodle, color, circle, underline, whatever will help your heart recall the promise it contains.

I have seen your salvation, which you have prepared for all people. He is a light to reveal God to the nations, and he is the glory of your people Israel.

Luke 2:30-32

Musical Notes "Messiah" by Francesca Battistelli

Final Thoughts _____
In light of today's devotion, share your own reflection or declaration:

Home _____

Hope _____

Hospitality _____

Hospitality
always demands
of us something.

Day Fifteen

Generosity Two Ways

When you start paying attention to the theme of hospitality in the Bible, it becomes hard to miss. Why, the chief commandments Jesus outlined for us underpin this. Love the Lord your God with all your heart, soul, mind and strength, and love your neighbor as yourself. Genuine *gospeltality* (to coin a Tim Keller phrase) is built upon these virtues. In the words of J.C. Ryle – "What we weave in time, we wear in eternity."

Hospitality always demands of us something. Money, time, energy—it never costs nothing at all. We open our homes, our pockets, our lives, especially in this Christmas season. Still, I want to encourage us in a type of lavishness that must never depart from our lives.

When I pulled my son aside to apologize for something I said too harshly, I was captivated by his gracious readiness to restore me almost before I could get the words out. That's just like a child, I'm sure you may say; but is that not the exact kingdom standard Jesus walked out and called us to? Isn't that the mercy we ourselves are afforded daily? Seventy times seven: that willingness to release each other when offenses do come. May our generosity overflow not just in giving, but in forgiving.

Prayerful Pause _____

Giver and Forgiver, may we excel in generosity not just in visible ways, but in the secret places of the heart. With myriad threads of forgiveness, may we tailor a cloak of righteousness that lasts through the ages. Amen.

A Good Word Matthew 18:21-22

Attention and Action ————————————————

• *Was one thought or phrase from today's devotional illuminated as you were reading? Jot it here and what it called to mind for you.*

• *Do you find it easy or difficult to apologize when you are wrong? What would help or has helped you grow in this area?*

• *Consider the thoughts and actions for which Christ has forgiven you. If you've anything to confess right now, ask His forgiveness below.*

• *Is there anyone who has hurt you or someone you love, that you are now willing to release into God's hands?*

Creative Meditation

Use this verse space to highlight key words, doodle, color, circle, underline, whatever will help your heart recall the promise it contains.

Then Peter came to him and asked, "Lord, how often should I forgive someone who sins against me? Seven times?" "No, not seven times," Jesus replied, "but seventy times seven! Matthew 18:21-22

Musical Notes "Silent Night" by 116 feat. Crystal Nicole

Final Thoughts

In light of today's devotion, share your own reflection or declaration:

Home

Hope

Hospitality

Take heart,
God reserves a
place of honor
for those found
blazing in the
background...

Day Sixteen
Prepare Him Room

If you could be any room in the house, which one would you choose? Depending on your personality you might choose a focal point like the living room, or maybe the master bedroom if you're more of an introvert. Or perhaps like me you'd like to be the kitchen—a space reminiscent of love, laughter, and of family gathering—a place that's wonderful smelling, with room for creativity, where it's ok to get a little messy. But have you considered the guest room? That sure can be a sought after space, even when people aren't visiting.

The trouble is this sacred sanctuary often leads a double life. Home office, makeshift laundry room, extra closet space, prayer room... it blends into the everyday as if it's nothing special. Yet its primary purpose cannot be detached. As fast as you can say "Welcome home!" that room is prepared to serve its distinct, uncommon function.

Are you feeling hidden, with untapped potential, or wonder if your daily efforts go unseen? Take heart! God reserves a place of honor for those found blazing in the background—men and women in obscurity, leading ordinary lives but living extraordinary love. They minister in the mundane and make the most of every opportunity. They rarely have the chance to shine, but are ready when it comes. Their faith's consistent glow will lead any weary traveler home.

Prayerful Pause

Oh God who sees, we are in good company with Simeon and Anna, Zechariah and Elizabeth, Mary and Joseph. They led faithful lives without seeking the spotlight, and so when the spotlight found them their character was not compromised. We can take up as little or as much space as you want us to, just make us vessels fit for Your use. Amen.

A Good Word 2 Timothy 2:20-21

Attention and Action ────────────────

• *Was one thought or phrase from today's devotional illuminated as you were reading? Jot it here and what it called to mind for you.*

• *Do you ever feel overlooked in service of God or others? Use God's promises as a reminder that you are seen and loved.*

• *Who do you know that could use your hands, heart or help within the next few days? Make a list and offer your services.*

• *Think of someone who leads an ordinary life but lives an extraordinary love. Have they any characteristics that you can mirror in your own life?*

Creative Meditation

Use this verse space to highlight key words, doodle, color, circle, underline, whatever will help your heart recall the promise it contains.

If you keep yourself pure, you will be a special utensil for honorable use. Your life will be clean, and you will be ready for the Master to use you for every good work. 2 Timothy 2:21

Musical Notes "Instruments of Your Peace (Prayer of St. Francis of Assisi)" by Rejoice Africa

Final Thoughts

In light of today's devotion, share your own reflection or declaration:

Home

Hope

Hospitality

Following Christ
will make us
uncomfortable.
And none of us is
so favored that
less would be
required.

Day Seventeen
Word Made Flesh

Dr. Luke discloses to us the transcript of a private conversation. Simeon is confirming the destiny of Jesus, prophesying the revelation that would come through this Living Word made flesh. He would be responsible for the rise and fall of many among God's people, and the thoughts of men's hearts would be revealed in the light of His presence. Finally, looking Mary right in the eyes, Simeon whispers these final words: "And a sword will pierce your own soul too." I can imagine her heart started to beat a little faster. Even the closest of relationships would not make her exempt from the hard things to come.

Have you ever read a book you could only bear a few pages at a time? Or listened to a podcast, the contents of which made you instantly squirm; not because it was something gory or unpleasant, but because you felt it calling you to a higher place of responsibility or action, demanding of you better character or behavior? In short, it made you uncomfortable. Following Christ will make us uncomfortable. And none of us is so favored that less would be required. What then are we to do?

We must thrust ourselves upon that double-edged sword that judges the thoughts and attitudes of our hearts, and allow His Living Word to be fleshed out in our lives. James says, *"For if anyone hears the word but is not obedient to it, he is like a man who looks at himself in a mirror and studies himself carefully, and then goes off and immediately forgets what he looks like."* But if we look closely into the perfect law that sets people free...if we pay attention and put it to practice, not listen and forget it—we will be blessed by God in what we do. It's when the Word becomes flesh and remains with us, that we see His glory, full of grace and truth.

Prayerful Pause

Lord, help us to flesh out in our lives the hard things of your Word, the gift of love You desire of us but never will demand. Help us follow obediently when the way may bring discomfort. Give us grace and vision as we wrestle with your Truth. Amen.

A Good Word James 1:23-25, John 1:14

Attention and Action

• *Was one thought or phrase from today's devotional illuminated as you were reading? Jot it here and what it called to mind for you.*

• *Which of God's commands do you find hardest to consistently carry out?*

• *When obedience is uncomfortable what helps you move from struggle to submission?*

• *Blessing comes not from being a hearer only, but a doer. What are you hearing today that you will step out and do?*

Creative Meditation

Use this verse space to highlight key words, doodle, color, circle, underline, whatever will help your heart recall the promise it contains.

So the Word became human and made his home among us. He was full of unfailing love and faithfulness. And we have seen his glory, the glory of the Father's one and only Son. John 1:14

Musical Notes "The Prayer" by Danny Gokey and Natalie Grant

Final Thoughts

In light of today's devotion, share your own reflection or declaration:

Home

Hope

Hospitality

It fixes its sights squarely on our Glorious King, Jesus, seems to take Him fully in, then out of the overflow of a heart full of worship, bows and magnifies Him.

Day Eighteen
Unveiled Faces

Oh come let us adore Him, for He alone is worthy, we'll give Him all the glory, Christ the Lord. It's one of those Christmas favorites that never disappoints. Sometimes it even makes the hair on my arms stand on end when I hear it. The song simply beams with majesty; its entrancing melody invites us to join in. But what I love most is simply the sense of honor it evokes. It fixes its sights squarely on our Glorious King, Jesus, seems to take Him fully in, then out of the overflow of a heart full of worship, bows and magnifies Him. And we get to sing along; each note inciting a new appreciation of His incomparable worth. I'm smiling just thinking about it.

What a wondrous gift we've been given—to see Him in His brilliance, to adore Him—for to see Him is to love Him, and fixing our eyes on Him helps us conform to His likeness. *"We all, who with unveiled faces contemplate the Lord's glory, are being transformed into His image with ever-increasing glory, which comes from the Lord, who is the Spirit,"* Apostle Paul mused.

Moses had to cover His face in order to encounter Him, but we've been granted access and fellowship with the Father through His Son... and so our joy is complete. Glory to God! Glory in the highest! O come let us adore Him, Christ the Lord.

Prayerful Pause _____

You are royalty. You have appeared to us. We marvel at Your great worth. We delight to worship You. Jesus, to Thee be all glory given. Amen.

A Good Word   2 Corinthians 3:18, 1 John 1:1

Attention and Action ―――――――――――――――

• *Was one thought or phrase from today's devotional illuminated as you were reading? Jot it here and what it called to mind for you.*

• *How precious to have been granted full and free access to such a great God through Jesus Christ! Share with Him what this means to you.*

• *Take some time to marvel at God's great worth. Try to use your own unique words and not someone else's language.*

• *End your devotion time with this song of worship to our God. Write down anything He speaks to your spirit.*

Creative Meditation _____

Use this verse space to highlight key words, doodle, color, circle, underline, whatever will help your heart recall the promise it contains.

We proclaim to you the one who existed from the beginning, whom we have heard and seen. We saw him with our own eyes and touched him with our own hands. He is the Word of life. 1 John 1:1

Gloria

Musical Notes "Oh Come" by Israel & New Breed

Final Thoughts _____

In light of today's devotion, share your own reflection or declaration:

Home _____

Hope _____

Hospitality _____

...everywhere we see Jesus appear,
women are close behind, and we see
Him celebrate and include them.

Day Nineteen

We Too

As I've held the Christmas story up to the light and turned it this way and that, something stood out to me that I didn't go looking for. Have you noticed that by biblical standards this story is chock full of women in such a small space? It's *only* three you may say, but tell me how often in the bible you see this many women in one narrative, in leading and supporting roles, taking up this much scriptural real estate—and acknowledged by name to boot.

These are multigenerational women from different walks and stages of life—differing demographics, overlapping paths. The story lends no masks to their pain, nor dampens their passion; it shows them in their weakness, their determination, innocence, foresight, fear, longing, acceptance. We see them overcome their struggles and run right into others. It shows their humanity, and at the same time, their hardiness. We see the impact of Jesus' coming on their lives.

This should be no surprise to us for everywhere we see Jesus appear, women are close behind, and we see Him celebrate and include them. Where tradition and 'isms' would oppress, we see Him elevate, affirm and bless. He takes their hands and leads them into positions 'reserved' for men only. He does not turn them away, but shields them and protects. They are allowed to approach Him boldly, and so they waste no time in worship. He regards them even in low estate – they are compelled to tell everyone about Him. They band His body in birth, and band it again in death, they are the first to know He is risen, and the first to share the good news. They are welcome at His table and at His wedding feast, as are we. The women our Lord encounters are marked by His kindness and validation; He invites us all in; and desires that not one be left outside.

Prayerful Pause

Thank you Lord, for redefining a woman's 'place' and always leading by example. You affirm and esteem us in love and truth, and lift us to belonging. Let all who seek You rejoice and be glad in You. Amen.

A Good Word Luke 1:45-49

Attention and Action

• *Was one thought or phrase from today's devotional illuminated as you were reading? Jot it here and what it called to mind for you.*

• *What is a woman's 'place' as defined by Jesus' example in the Gospels? How does this reflect the heart of the Father for His daughters?*

• *How can women support the cause of Christ in a modern day context and so partner with their sisters who walked with Him in real time?*

• *Take some time to pray for the faithful females around you. Thank God for the gift they are to your life.*

Creative Meditation _____

Use this verse space to highlight key words, doodle, color, circle, underline, whatever will help your heart recall the promise it contains.

"You are blessed because you believed that the Lord would do what he said." Mary responded, "Oh, how my soul praises the Lord. How my spirit rejoices in God my Savior! For he took notice of his lowly servant..."

Luke 1:46-48a

Musical Notes "The Proof of Your Love" by for KING & COUNTRY featuring Rebecca St. James

Final Thoughts _____

In light of today's devotion, share your own reflection or declaration:

Home _____

Hope _____

Hospitality _____

...promises and covenants and good men with good character cannot save us from the death that sin introduced into the world.

Day Twenty
Fathering Nations

Joseph has always intrigued me. So little is said about him, yet his uncompromising character and its resulting imprint in Jesus' life are evident. We learn of his careful treatment of his betrothed, even before he was cautioned not to break off the engagement. We see his courage in the face of fear, and His willingness to obey God. We see Him take up responsibility that he could easily have lain down, and do everything he can to protect and do right by his beloved ones. He is a good father—so present and recognizable in Jesus' life that Mary chides Him when she thinks His actions may have hurt Joseph. Later on Jesus is well known as *the carpenter's son*. No better man could have fathered this young King.

Jesus wasn't part of Joseph's biological bloodline, yet Matthew lists Joseph's full genealogy. Why would he run through a smooth list of *begats* to almost stammer at the end trying to properly define their relationship? The names tell a tale of promise. God told Abraham that in his seed all the nations of the earth would be blessed. To David He promises there will be no end to the increase of his government or of peace on his throne, and over his kingdom, to establish it with justice and righteousness, forever.

Still, promises and covenants and good men with good character cannot save us from the death that sin introduced into the world. This could only happen through a sinless Savior. Jesus came, separate by virgin birth from the tarnished bloodline, but fulfilling under Joseph's legal custody the promises to his ancestry...and so we too have been grafted in. A Son was given and the government now rests on His shoulders; our salvation, Hope of Nations and He shall reign forever and ever.

Prayerful Pause _____

Mighty King, Your kingdom and its increase shall know no end. We hide and abide in all that You've done to save us from sin's wages. You live, now so do we. Amen.

A Good Word Isaiah 9:2-3,6-7

Attention and Action ————————————————

• *Was one thought or phrase from today's devotional illuminated as you were reading? Jot it here and what it called to mind for you.*

• *Think of some ways that Joseph's fathering shows up in Jesus's life, and note them here.*

• *Our families of origin hold tremendous significance whether or not we know their history. How has what you know of your family affected your life?*

• *We are grafted into Jesus's gene pool through His sacrifice on the cross. This can't change your past; in what ways does it change your present?*

Creative Meditation _____

Use this verse space to highlight key words, doodle, color, circle, underline, whatever will help your heart recall the promise it contains.

For to us a child is born, to us a son is given, and the government will be on his shoulders. And he will be called Wonderful Counselor, Mighty God, Everlasting Father, Prince of Peace. Isaiah 9:6

Musical Notes "Hope of Nations" by Gates Praise

Final Thoughts _____

In light of today's devotion, share your own reflection or declaration:

Home _____

Hope _____

Hospitality _____

He always
surprises
me how He
shows up,
where, and
when, and
through
whom.

Day Twenty-one
A Table Prepared

The people of Israel were looking for a Priest and King, they were longing for a Messiah; for one who would come and deliver them from enemy oppression. What they weren't looking for, nor knew they needed, was the kind of Messiah Jesus would be: one who would ultimately save them not from subjugation to earthly powers alone, but from spiritual wickedness and the power of sin, death, hell and the grave. The book of Romans tells us that while we were yet sinners, Christ died for us. We see this common thread of our Mighty God meeting the needs we have, even before we recognise our great poverty of heart and soul.

At a time like Christmas when so often we are focused on our wants, God is still fixed on the rich supply of our needs—spiritual, emotional, mental, physical. His Word reminds us He has already given us everything we need for life and godliness, and He shall continually supply all our needs according to His riches in glory—the ones that persist, the ones we don't even know we have, the ones to come.

He always surprises me how He shows up, where, and when, and through whom. In fact, you may just be that point of supply for someone else. He is a table prepared, Bread of Life in a feeding trough, Living Water at a well, Choice Wine poured out, Miraculous Bountiful Supply to meet us where we are at. Come feast, all you who have nothing but your lives to offer. Our God knows our needs and will supply them ALL.

Prayerful Pause

Lord we number not our needs for we know You know them all. Yet sometimes we need to be reminded that You have everything in control. This Christmas we lay our burdens down and replace them with Your light and easy yoke with gratefulness. Amen.

A Good Word Romans 5:8, Isaiah 55:1-2

Attention and Action _____

• *Was one thought or phrase from today's devotional illuminated as you were reading? Jot it here and what it called to mind for you.*

• *List a few things you found in Jesus that you never realized you needed before you met Him.*

• *What are some needs—spiritual, emotional, mental, physical—that you are trusting God to provide today?*

• *Might He want to show up as a meeter of needs for someone else through you? Ask Him to show you who and how you can help, and then take action.*

Creative Meditation

Use this verse space to highlight key words, doodle, color, circle, underline, whatever will help your heart recall the promise it contains.

"Is anyone thirsty? Come and drink—even if you have no money! Come, take your choice of wine or milk—it's all free! Why spend your money on food that does not give you strength?" Isaiah 55:1-2a

Musical Notes "Real Love" by 116 feat. Itstaylormade, Wande and Byron Juane

Final Thoughts

In light of today's devotion, share your own reflection or declaration:

Home

Hope

Hospitality

Jesus came to bring us out of alienation and into His glorious Kingdom.

Day Twenty-two
Homeward Bound

In my island, Barbados, a promotion called *Home for the Holidays* was run by a local radio station. It reunited Bajans within the diaspora with loved ones back home. Generally, many years had elapsed since they had last seen and held each other. The airport arrival scenes were tearjerkers—there's just something about being home.

The word *diaspora* by definition recalls the exile of the Jews scattered from their homeland centuries ago. Forced to live captive in foreign lands, away from what was familiar and secure, hope waned for the possibility of returning. And yet they did, in waves and over a long period, in depleted numbers and with emaciated spirits, they stumbled back to the place of their birth. Their land had been restored, but they'd come back to a mere shadow of what they'd been forced from. In need of leadership and fortitude they longed for something more. As do we, who recognise that this world is hostile territory.

Exile is not just the problem of people groups, but the status of all human beings. Jesus came to bring us out of alienation and into His glorious Kingdom. He loves the homeless, the wanderer, the disenfranchised and the squatter. He knows what it's like. After all, He Himself stepped out of His own home, and into a hostile territory where He had no place to lay His head.

He goes to the fringes to make sure that not one is left out. He calls all that will come, but especially the overlooked, the least, the ostracised, the 'freaks', the lowest castes, the broken, the outcast, the shepherds and the one lost sheep. He's come for you and me, and He says, "I'm preparing a place for you."

Prayerful Pause

Even so, come Lord Jesus. You are our cornerstone, our walls and our sure foundation. Thank you for having a plan that covers us. May we all feel at home in Your love. Amen.

A Good Word John 14:2, Luke 15:4

Attention and Action ——————————————

• *Was one thought or phrase from today's devotional illuminated as you were reading? Jot it here and what it called to mind for you.*

• *Society assigns people with labels, but God calls us accepted because of Christ's sacrifice. Thank Him here for that great gift of worth.*

• *People suffer with feelings of rejection all the time. If it's not you, it may be someone you know. Note a few ways you can remind them they are loved.*

• *Does home feel like a safe space for you and your family right now? Is there anything you can do to make it more secure?*

Creative Meditation _____

Use this verse space to highlight key words, doodle, color, circle, underline, whatever will help your heart recall the promise it contains.

If a man has a hundred sheep and one of them gets lost, what will he do? Won't he leave the ninety-nine others in the wilderness and go to search for the one that is lost until he finds it?

Luke 15:4

Musical Notes "Least of These" by Israel & New Breed

Final Thoughts _____

In light of today's devotion, share your own reflection or declaration:

Home _____

Hope _____

Hospitality _____

The light isn't intimidated by the darkness, it just breaks right through.

Day Twenty-three

Burn More Than Candles

Been doing some late night painting. Neatened my desk, took up my rinse water, and my artwork to go scan it, along with an armful of other items. Flipped off the light. You may know where this is going... Forgot the pouffe in the middle of the family room, fell right over it, wet nostrils, two bruises and a crack in my screen protector to show for it. Light is essential for sight; who knew? It never once occurred to me that something would obstruct my path. But there it was, hidden in the darkness waiting (proverbially) to take me out.

Life can feel like stumbling around in an unlit room. We trust our own instincts and try to navigate the terrain—running through the rituals, checking off the boxes, straight shot through to the other side. We hold our breath hoping all will go well, and nothing will spring out of nowhere to offset the delicate balance. Yet we needn't; the Light of the World came to illuminate our lives and help us to see clearly. The light isn't intimidated by the darkness, it just breaks right through. May it always lead us in the way we should go.

But Jesus turns the beam and says we too are the light of the world. If I believe His Word, I understand that I am a city built on the mount that is Christ—a beacon of hope, deliverance and direction. I have elevation I know not of, a unique perspective and experiential vantage point for sharing His truth come alive. If my foundations are in Christ, being a witness to His light is my glory. It is the purpose for which I was built, even when I am afraid, or feel like I don't know enough, and though it may cost my reputation or my life. I was designed to be set on fire for Him, and for that fire to never go out. That my life be a light; I must allow it first to burn.

Prayerful Pause

Light of the World, we desire that our lives and our lips would lead others to You. Even amidst the busyness may we seek opportunity to set other hearts ablaze with the fire of Your love. Amen.

A Good Word Matthew 5:14-16; Leviticus 6:13

Attention and Action ───────────────

• *Was one thought or phrase from today's devotional illuminated as you were reading? Jot it here and what it called to mind for you.*

• *Are there any dim or dark areas of your life where God is shining His light so that you will no longer stumble?*

• *What do you know of Christ from personal experience that others would benefit from hearing about? In other words, what is your testimony?*

• *What are some practical ways in which we can keep the fire of God's love burning in our hearts?*

Creative Meditation _____

Use this verse space to highlight key words, doodle, color, circle, underline, whatever will help your heart recall the promise it contains.

In the same way, let your good deeds shine out for all to see, so that everyone will praise your heavenly Father.

Matthew 5:16

Musical Notes "Light of the World" by Lauren Daigle

Final Thoughts _____

In light of today's devotion, share your own reflection or declaration:

Home _____

Hope _____

Hospitality _____

He has etched
us into eternity,
masterful
creations, glory
fading fast.

Day Twenty-Four
Finishing Touches

Now let's end where we began. On Day One we talked about snowflakes and the extravagance of our God. These tiny flecks of ice each bear the carvings of a Divine Craftsman; not one like the other, perfectly executed, each one a wonder. Yet, because their true intricacies aren't visible to the naked eye, most will never be fully recognized or appreciated. Think how many of these masterpieces get crushed underfoot, scraped off windshields, mixed in with the slush on busy city streets. It brings the Creator joy to etch them anyway. To Him they are still purposeful, and down to the last detail worth the breadth of their existence, however frail, however brief.

In much the same way, He has etched us into eternity, masterful creations, glory fading fast. Each one of us uniquely fashioned down to our very fingerprints, with our DNA a signature of loving precision. There are aspects of our beings that another man may never excavate, preserved in privacy for His enjoyment alone. So, He makes His mark on the human heart, devoted to completing the good work He has begun in us.

Humanity was the mould Divinity poured Himself into; so through the person of Jesus Christ He can put on us His finishing touches. To Him we are that purposeful, and down to the last detail worth every breath of His existence, however frail, however brief. Thanks be to God for His indescribable gift!

Prayerful Pause

God who knows us through and through, unremoved from His creation. You've made a birth announcement into a wedding invitation, and will present us to Yourself without spot or wrinkle. And so for all these things we give You thanks. Amen.

A Good Word Isaiah 62:5; Ephesians 5:27

Attention and Action

• *Was one thought or phrase from today's devotional illuminated as you were reading? Jot it here and what it called to mind for you.*

• *What are the unique qualities that make you a masterful creation? He took His time with you. Take your time with this exercise.*

• *Describe how this devotional time with Holy Spirit has brought you closer to Him and others.*

• *Express your joy and gratitude that the work He has begun in you, He is faithful to finish.*

Creative Meditation

Use this verse space to highlight key words, doodle, color, circle, underline, whatever will help your heart recall the promise it contains.

Your children will commit themselves to you, O Jerusalem, just as a young man commits himself to his bride. Then God will rejoice over you as a bridegroom rejoices over his bride. Isaiah 62:5

Musical Notes "Joy To The World (Joyful, Joyful)" by Phil Wickham

Final Thoughts

In light of today's devotion, share your own reflection or declaration:

Home

Hope

Hospitality

Warm Thanks

Thank you for accepting this invitation to our table, for breaking bread with us over the past 24 days. Receive this blessing as we rise to leave.

For God is the one who provides seed for the farmer and then bread to eat. In the same way, he will provide and increase your resources and then produce a great harvest of generosity in you.

Yes, you will be enriched in every way so that you can always be generous. And when we take your gifts to those who need them, they will thank God. So two good things will result from this ministry of giving—the needs of the believers in Jerusalem will be met, and they will joyfully express their thanks to God.

As a result of your ministry, they will give glory to God. For your generosity to them and to all believers will prove that you are obedient to the Good News of Christ. And they will pray for you with deep affection because of the overflowing grace God has given to you. Thank God for this gift too wonderful for words!

2 Corinthians 9:10-15

Musical Notes "This is Jesus" by We Are Messengers

About the Author

Tao Howard's passion for words has been a constant companion since childhood expressing itself in stacks of diaries, an obsession with spelling, scripture memorization and reading everything including the back of the toothpaste tube. In her teenage years in Barbados, art, language and literature made up much of her studies and she developed a love for poetry. Some of her own poems received NIFCA literary awards and were published in that body's Winning Words Anthology. Other of her collections are yet to be published.

She pivoted to claim her first degree in Tourism Management with First Class Honors and after working a few years in the industry she was able to marry her love for hospitality and appreciation for books and design at a local publishing company. That has led to over a decade of experience in publication design, graphic design and branding.

Tao Howard is a multifaceted 'generalist', with a unique combination of creative skills. She is an entrepreneur, blogger and writer, an ordained and licensed minister with Christian International Apostolic Network, and a John Maxwell certified communicator. She relishes opportunities to support others in understanding who they are, maximizing their potential, and growing beyond their goals. Her public instagram profile @itspronouncedtao shares meaningful thoughts and encouragement, while her monthly newsletter and blog helps others mine for everyday magic in the mundane. Tao has contributed as a guest writer to other online Christian publications, and engaged in various copywriting and editing opportunities. She has a voracious appetite to develop in the art and science of writing and happily shares her knowledge with author friends and clients whose books she produces.

She and her husband, Dwayne, co-direct Kainos Creative Studios Inc. (@kainoscreates) and co-founded Awake the Flame Ministries (@awake.the.flame) bridging the gap between marketplace and ministry daily. Kainos is a creative firm offering multi-platform design services, directed at helping clients soar above the best. Awake the Flame is a family founded global apostolic/prophetic ministry called to awaken a passion for Jesus in the nations. Dwayne and Tao co-labour in oversight and service of both organizations while juggling personal, family and business responsibilities. They are the proud parents of three active and outstanding sons.

Get in Touch

Publishing/Permissions tao@kainoscs.com

Newsletter itspronouncedtao.substack.com
Blog itspronouncedtao.wordpress.com
Instagram/Facebook @itspronouncedtao

Ministry/Speaking Engagements tao@awaketheflame.com

Printed in Dunstable, United Kingdom